Take the ***A****dventure &* ***E****xplore*

by Scott R. Kudelka

Adventure Publications, Inc.
Cambridge, Minnesota

DEDICATION

To my partner and best friend, Angie, who inspired me to write this book!

To my parents, Roger and Shirley, who have always believed in me.

This book is for my niece, Jenny Kudelka Hanson, as she begins to explore and enjoy her own adventures in North Dakota.

Edited by Hope Klocker and Brett Ortler

Book and cover design by Jonathan Norberg

Photo Credits by photographer and page number:
Cover photo: Swimming beach by North Dakota Parks and Recreation
Angie Becker Kudelka: 80 **Scott R. Kudelka:** 8, 9, 13, 14, 15, 17, 18, 19, 20, 21, 22, 23, 24, 25, 29, 33, 34, 38, 39, 40, 41, 42, 43, 44, 45, 46, 56, 57, 60, 61, 62, 63, 64, 65, 66 **Shirley Kudelka:** 4, 5 **North Dakota Parks and Recreation:** 10, 11, 16, 26, 28, 30, 31, 32, 35, 36, 40, 44, 49, 50, 51, 53, 54, 55, 57, 58, 59, 67, 68, 69, 70, 71

10 9 8 7 6 5 4 3 2 1
Copyright 2008 by Scott R. Kudelka
Published by Adventure Publications, Inc.
820 Cleveland St. S
Cambridge, MN 55008
1-800-678-7006
www.adventurepublications.net
All rights reserved
Printed in China
ISBN-13: 978-1-59193-184-3
ISBN-10: 1-59193-184-3

ACKNOWLEDGMENTS

Where do I start? Well, I want to thank and acknowledge everyone for the help they gave me in putting this book series together. First off, a big thank you to my family for their support, excitement and assistance with the creation of the North Dakota State Parks set of guidebooks.

I want to especially thank Doug Prchal and Donna Schouweiler with the North Dakota Parks and Recreation Department for their ongoing encouragement with this project and their support with the accuracy of the material. As I traveled across the state acquiring images, a number of people went out of their way to help me. This includes Henry Duray, Lorraine Schroeder and Dennis Clark at Icelandic State Park; Jim Loken at Beaver Lake State Park; Maureen Trnka and Dan Schelske at Fort Abraham Lincoln State Park; John Kwapinski at Fort Ransom State Park; Dick Messerly of Fort Stevenson State Park; Steve Crandall at Turtle River State Park; Larry Hagen and Bill Deming at Lake Metigoshe State Park; Eric Lang at Cross Ranch State Park; Dick Horner of Devils Lake; John Tunge of Lake Sakakawea and the staff of Lewis and Clark State Park. Thanks also to Erik Spencer, Mark Brown and Kris Dirk for help with maps and photos.

Thanks to Kelly Sorge for providing material and photos on Indian Hills State Recreation Area. From the North Dakota Game and Fish Department it was Dale Repnow, Brian Prince, Bruce Renhowe, Dan Halstead and Craig Bihrle; at the U.S. Forest Service it was Darla Lenz; and material on the U.S. Fish and Wildlife Service was reviewed by Ken Torkelson, Jackie Jacobson, Lynda Knutsen, Ted Gutzke, Joe Maxwell, Paul Halko and Dean Knauer. At the Lewis and Clark Interpretive Center it was Kevin Kirkey. From North Dakota Tourism, I want to thank James (Scooter) Pursley for help with their photo collection. Thanks also to Kit and Fay Henegar of Captain Kit's Marina.

Finally, I need to thank everyone at Adventure Publications for giving me this great opportunity. It is an experience that will stay with me forever. Thanks especially to my long-suffering and dedicated editors, Hope Klocker and Brett Ortler.

I grew up in southeastern North Dakota in a town of 500 or so people. Forman sits on the edge of the Red River Valley, close enough to see the rich agricultural land but stuck with a rockier terrain. My parents enjoyed throwing us kids in the back of a cramped camper on a 1960 green Ford pickup in search of a new adventure. Some of our best trips unfolded within North Dakota's borders. This was a great way to explore our home state and experience the unique characteristics of a prairie landscape.

Vivid memories of visiting state and national parks as a young boy still fill my head. The big trip of my youth was to the Badlands at around age eight, exploring a crumbling landscape where Theodore Roosevelt rediscovered his passion after the death of his wife and mother. In the various state parks, I pretended to be one of Custer's cavalry at the blockhouses of Fort McKeen, skateboarded along the rolling, curving roads in the riparian (floodplain) ecosystem of Turtle River and roasted marshmallows at Fort Stevenson Recreation Area before it became a state park. I also scrambled up the steep Pyramid Hill near Ransom for a close-up view of the Viking statue; saw my breath on a cold morning at Icelandic and discovered aquatic life in creeks flowing into the Sheyenne River.

Author at Little Missouri State Park

In the summer of 1986, I got thrown into the job of seasonal park ranger at Little Missouri Bay State Park, straddling the line between the Great Plains and Badlands. With no clue what this job was all about, I saw it as a once-in-a-lifetime experience. As the only employee of a 5,000-plus-acre park, this lifestyle charmed me and it didn't let go until the end of the century, when I finished my parks career as a full-time ranger. In between, I bounced around North Dakota working at Fort Stevenson, Cross Ranch, Lake Metigoshe and Icelandic. During that time I cross-country skied 104 days during the severe winter of 1996-97, helped build the Centennial Log Cabin at Cross Ranch and never took my service revolver out of its holster.

This book is a result of the work I did during my 15 years in the Parks and Recreation Department. A number of good people crossed my path in my life as a park ranger and played a major influence. Daryl Kleyer, a Sakakawea park ranger, took a chance on me more than once and gave me the job at Little Missouri Bay. Jesse Hanson, brother-in-law, mentor and the guy who introduced me to the Hensler Bar. Jesse and my sister, Lisa, always had a bed, meal and job when I was down on my luck. Doug Prchal was my late-night philosopher buddy and horse wrangler. Jim Loken, the one guy who believed I could soar higher than as a seasonal ranger at Fort Stevenson. Brad Pozarnsky, who allowed me to fly without boundaries. And Dennis Clark, Kevin Kirkey and Darla Lenz, three of my best friends, who were always willing to hear my stories and ramblings of life. To my brother, Brian, and my sister, Susan, who shared some of my best experiences exploring the state parks of North Dakota. Finally, to Chris, my other brother-in-law, who survived a chaotic 6-hour canoe trip on the Sheyenne River.

Author and father in the Badlands

TABLE OF CONTENTS

INTRODUCTION

Nestled along a sandy ridge of the former glacial Lake Agassiz, Icelandic State Park sits at the edge of the remains of the once far-reaching tallgrass prairie. While the name of the park recognizes the area's significance as a major destination for Icelandic pioneers, it also celebrates a diverse selection of ethnic groups making their home here in northeastern North Dakota.

This 912-acre park features Lake Renwick, the Gunlogson Nature Preserve, Pioneer Heritage Center complex and Pioneer Machinery Site. Located 20 miles from the Canadian border, Icelandic provides a number of recreational, interpretive and cultural opportunities.

Park Entrance

The formation of the park started with the construction of Renwick Dam in 1959. Lake Renwick was created to control flooding along the Tongue River after a number of devastating floods in the late 1940s and early '50s. It was the last in a series of seven dams built in the region by the federal government's Small Watershed Program. This 220-acre lake came under the control of Pembina County's Water Management Board, which developed a recreation area for the public. Renwick became a popular spot for pleasure boaters, water-skiers, anglers and campers.

An important feature of Icelandic State Park is the Gunlogson Homestead and Nature Preserve. In 1964, Gunnlauger Biarni (G.B.) and Loa Gunlogson donated their parents' farm and 200 acres to the North Dakota Park Service. On August 25, 1978, a 94-acre section of Gunlogson's original homestead was dedicated as North Dakota's first nature preserve. This unique area along the Tongue River is home to a wide range of plants and animals, with several classified as threatened or rare in the state. One of very few spots left virtually undisturbed, today the Gunlogson Nature Preserve provides an excellent opportunity to view and study a variety of natural communities largely untouched by the human race.

The park is well known for its historical interpretation, including the Pioneer Heritage Center Complex. Built to tell the story of the first settlers, it now includes the Hallson Church, Cranley School, Akra Hall and a log cabin. Other historical resources in the park include the Pioneer Machinery Site—home to the Bathgate Depot—Stegman Barn, and the newly constructed Pembina County Museum. There are Red River oxcart trails still in evidence and an old sheepherder's site on the edge of the Gunlogson Homestead.

Outside of Icelandic State Park, nature and wildlife lovers should check out two great areas. To the northwest, Jay V. Wessels Wildlife Management Area offers a habitat for large mammals like moose and game birds ranging from ruffed grouse to wild turkeys. Along the Canadian border is the Pembina Gorge, featuring a steep terrain normally not associated with North Dakota; it includes a great river to canoe and heavily forested landscape filled with wildlife. Look for a large elk herd moving back and forth between the state and Canada. There are also a number of major historic sites to visit, including the Pembina State Museum and Gingras Trading Post.

Pembina River

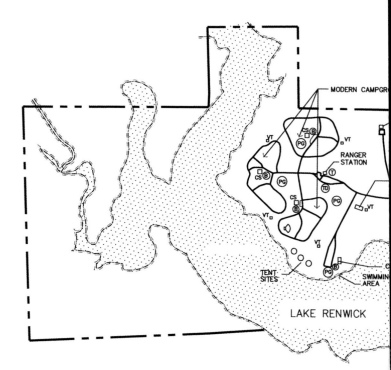

MODERN CAMPGR

RANGER
STATION

TENT
SITES

SWIMMIN
AREA

LAKE RENWICK

CAVALIER
COUNTRY
CLUB

LEGEND

□ CS   COMFORT STATION
ⓣⒹ   DUMP STATION
□ VT   VAULT TOILET
⌐   BUILDING
Ⓣ   PAY PHONE
Ⓑ   BULLETIN BOARD
ⓅⒼ   PLAYGROUND
♗   AMPHITHEATER

– – – – – – –   TRAILS

——— — — —   PARK BOUNDARY

—— ·· —— ·· ——   LAKE/RIVER BOUNDARY

SCALE: 1"= 800'

0'   400'   800'

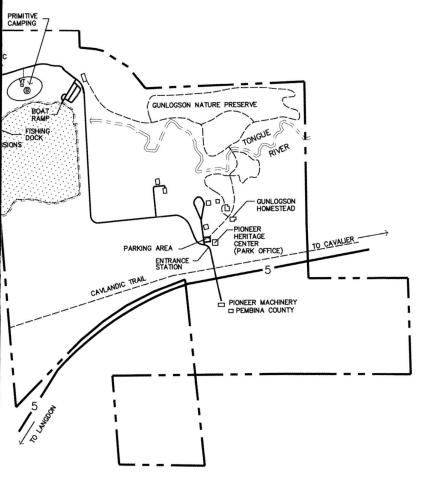

—150 SITES

MAINTENANCE AREA

PRIMITIVE CAMPING

BOAT RAMP

FISHING DOCK

GUNLOGSON NATURE PRESERVE

TONGUE RIVER

GUNLOGSON HOMESTEAD

PARKING AREA

PIONEER HERITAGE CENTER (PARK OFFICE)

ENTRANCE STATION

TO CAVALIER

5

CAVLANDIC TRAIL

PIONEER MACHINERY
PEMBINA COUNTY

5
TO LANGDON

PARK AT A GLANCE

Location/Directions 5.5 miles west of Cavalier on Hwy. 5, between Hwys. 32 and 18.

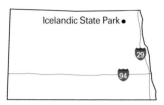

From Grand Forks take I-29 north for 66 miles to exit 203 and turn west on Hwy. 81; this turns into Hwy. 5, traveling a total of 14.5 miles to the park.

This state park is located near the Canadian border and the city of Winnipeg, Manitoba. It is south of Walhalla and east of Langdon.

Contact Information

13571 Hwy. 5, Cavalier, ND 58220; 701-265-4561; isp@nd.gov

Established 1964

Size 912 acres of bottomland and native prairie along the Tongue River and Lake Renwick

Visitor Services

- Pioneer Heritage Center
- historic buildings: Akra Hall, Cranley School, Hallson Church, log cabin
- Gunlogson house and homestead
- Pembina County Museum and Pioneer Machinery Site
- Gunlogson Nature Preserve and hiking trails
- multi-purpose non-motorized path
- special events
- meeting rooms and kitchen facilities
- interpretive and educational programs
- Lake Renwick and fishing dock
- swimming beach and concessions

- sleeping cabins
- campgrounds
- picnic shelter and playgrounds
- winter activities

Camping
- 159 RV and tent sites open year-round

Playground

Things You'll Want To Do

- Enjoy the park's modern campground, its picnic shelters, playground and take advantage of the hiking trails as well as the self-guided nature trails.

- Step back in time as you see the many historic buildings including Akra Hall, Cranley School, Hallson Church, the Gunlogson House and Homestead and the Pembina County Museum and Pioneer Machinery Site.

- Visit Pioneer Heritage Center and immerse yourself in the history of the region; learn about everything from pioneer life to the region's geological history.

- Paddle through the scenic Pembina Gorge west of Walhalla on the Pembina River, the only whitewater stream in North Dakota.

- Enjoy the winter season by ice fishing on Lake Renwick, taking a wild ride on the sledding hill, or cross-country skiing in the Tongue River riparian (floodplain) area.

PIONEER HERITAGE COMPLEX

This collection of historical buildings tells the story of North Dakota's early homesteading years and the immense impact of these immigrants, through artifacts, exhibits, historical buildings, personal stories, hands-on displays and audio-visual programs. First envisioned by G.B. Gunlogson in the 1960s, this complex teaches visitors about the life of pioneers and their eye-opening accomplishments. Experience the Settlement Story of 1870 to 1920 through a heritage center, one-room school, a community hall, pioneer church, log cabin and Gunlogson homestead. This complex is unique because it isn't a museum; each building can be used for special events, dances, family reunions, church services, weddings, fashion shows and classroom events. Call the park for current rental fees and provisions.

Pioneer Heritage Center

This interpretive center teaches visitors about the history of the northeast region. Visitors learn about many different topics, everything from how glaciers created Lake Agassiz to what it took to build a new settlement. An addition to the building will include more exhibit space, a larger store and a permanent exhibit about the Gunlogson Nature Preserve.

Built in 1989 to celebrate the state centennial and G.B. Gunlogson's vision of telling the story of the early pioneers

Pioneer Heritage Center

Hours summer 9–9 daily; off-season Sun 1–5, Mon-Fri 9–5

Facilities gift store, temporary display area, two meeting rooms (which can accommodate up to 50 people), research room, library and restrooms

Programs special events, temporary exhibits, audio-visual programs and guest speakers

Gunlogson Homestead

Eggert and Rannveig Gunnlaugson (Gunlogson) emigrated from their native Iceland in 1876. Harsh conditions at home led the Gunnlaugsons and many other Icelanders to seek a better life in the New World. After trying their luck in Canada, the family moved to this site along the Tongue

Gunlogson House

River to start a new life in the spring of 1880. Their first home was a log cabin built by Eggert.

Built 1882-1890. Later, a summer kitchen was added. The house consists of five rooms on the main floor, one room upstairs, an attic and a cellar. The youngest daughter, Loa, was the last person to live in the house.

Hours spring through early fall for individual and group tours

Other Buildings include a barn, outhouse, storage shed, granary and garage (a second granary was destroyed in a tornado, although the foundation remains).

Gunlogson Barn was renovated into a nature center with wildlife exhibits

Cranley School

Representing the 102 rural schools once found in Pembina County, it helped educate a number of young pioneers. Education was vitally important to the early settlers, who were seeking a better life for themselves and their children.

School class at Cranley School

Built in 1881 on land donated by Michael Cranley north and east of Cavalier. There were 32 pupils of all ages and backgrounds. The school closed on June 15, 1959, and annexed with the Cavalier School System. It was used for storage until Floyd Helgoe donated it to the Heritage Association in 1987.

Dedicated September 13, 1992, after two years of reconstruction.

Hours May–Sept for school days, individual and group tours and other events. Offers one-room, turn-of-the century schoolhouse with chalkboards, books, desks and bell.

Akra Hall

The community hall played an important role in the life of early settlers. Social events were a time for people to put their daily lives aside to gather as a community. Dances, card tournaments, community suppers, elections and talent shows were just some of the activities that took place in these halls.

Built 1901 in the small village of Akra, a mile east of the Gunlogson homestead, by the Modern Woodmen of America. The last dance was held in the 1960s and the hall was later purchased by the Abrahamson brothers. They donated it to the Heritage Association in 1987.

Dedicated on August 21, 1994, with Chuck Suchy, North Dakota's troubadour, entertaining a large crowd. An entryway with modern kitchen and bathroom facilities was added later.

Akra Hall

Hours Year-round for public events including family reunions, dances and other celebrations; spring through fall for tours. Includes a spacious kitchen, modern bathrooms, dressing rooms and exhibit area. Rental includes chairs, tables and kitchenware.

Pioneer Log Cabin

This final component of the complex represents the traditional home built by pioneers as they settled the area.

Built Started in 1996 and finished in 2000, when it was dedicated.

Pioneer Log Cabin

Hallson Church

One of the original Icelandic immigrants, Johann P. Hallson, established a village site along the Tongue River west of the park. Religion was an important aspect for these pioneers, with the construction of a church as one of the first community buildings. This building includes an altar area, pews, organ, Bibles, hymnals and a working bell and is available for private use April through October.

Hours year-round for public events; spring through early fall for tours

Built 1887 on land donated by Johann Hallson along with labor, bell, pastor's chair, altar and pulpit. The congregation celebrated its anniversary in 1986 and agreed to move the church to the park.

Dedicated First in 1889 during the annual Icelandic Lutheran Synod convention. The second dedication occurred during the summer of 1997 after a generous donation by the Alfred Bryon family to restore the church, including original bell tower.

Hallson Church

PIONEER MACHINERY SITE

Created in the early 1990s to display the equipment used by the original pioneers of Pembina County. Located south of the Pioneer Heritage Center within Icelandic State Park, it is managed by the Pembina County Historical Society. Currently, the site features the Pembina County Museum, Bathgate Depot, McKechnie Granary, Stegman Barn, Paton House and a number of display buildings. A recent addition is the large, wooden St. Anthony Catholic Church. The site hosts the annual Pioneer Machinery Day and the Rendezvous Festival.

Hours 1–5 daily, Memorial Day through second weekend of September

Pembina County Museum

This 8,400-square-foot museum introduces visitors to the story of Pembina County and other buildings on the site. A permanent exhibit area tells the history through a discussion of religion, education, communities, businesses, agriculture, recreation, military and other topics.

Features permanent artifact collection, research library, temporary display gallery, meeting room and store

Bathgate Depot

A train depot was the heart of rural communities like Bathgate. As with most other small towns, the railroad was its connection to the rest of the world. It was the place where you could send a

Bathgate Depot

telegram, pick up a family member, or ship farm products. For decades it served as one of the more important community buildings. This changed as cars, trucks and buses took on a greater role in the transportation of people and goods.

Features variety of railroad artifacts, the Barry Historical Collection and a meeting room

Display Buildings

These three 60' x 100' buildings hold a selection of historical artifacts collected throughout Pembina County. This includes vehicles of all ages and types, along with machinery and farm tools.

A fourth display building holds the 2-cylinder Fairbanks-Morse engine that once supplied power for the city of Cavalier.

McKechnie Granary

A granary was extremely important to the pioneers because it stored the fruits of their hard work and provided security for the future. This unique building has an oak beam infrastructure that is exceptionally rare. Originally located next to the Cavalier School, it is the oldest known city structure. After the building fell into disrepair, the McKechnie family donated it to the Pembina County Historical Society in 1996 and paid for the reconstruction work. This building represents the ingenuity of the early pioneers.

Stegman Barn

One of the first buildings constructed on a farm, barns were built to protect valuable livestock including horses and cows. In addition, barns stored hay and grain for the livestock. Barns were also important for recreational activities, including the all-important Saturday night dances.

Stegman Barn and Blacksmith Shop

The Stegman Barn was built in 1936 and represents the typical farm building of its day. Donated by Mark and Russell Stegman, the newly restored barn features lanterns, shovels, wheelbarrows, harnesses, hoof trimmers and milk stools.

Paton House

Built in the late 1800s, the Paton House represents a typical pioneer homesteader's first home, a wooden structure that was simple and inexpensive to build. Many of these original homes were crowded with large, extended families.

Paton House

Adam Currie Paton (1846–1943) built the house after immigrating to the area from Canada. It had been preserved by the family at Paton's Isle of Memories as one of the original homesteads in the Park Center area. The Wilbur Paton family donated the house to the Pembina County Historical Society in his memory.

St. Anthony's Catholic Church

The oldest original frame church in North Dakota, built in 1882–'83 along the Tongue River in Bathgate. Over the years, there had been a number of improvements, although when floodwaters were high it made for an adventurous walk to the church.

As the rural population declined, the church membership fell sharply, leading to a decision to preserve the structure by donating it to the Pembina County Historical Society. In late fall of 2002 the building was moved to the Pioneer Machinery Site.

St Anthony's Catholic Church

FACILITIES

Campground Area

Visitors will find this area of the park spacious and heavily forested with both conifers and deciduous trees, providing privacy for the sites. Facilities range from simple sleeping cabins to a well-placed fishing dock. On most weekends during the summer, parking is often a challenge at the beach area.

- full service from weekend before Memorial Day to end of September
- limited service available year-round
- during summer contact campground hosts, at beginning of west loop of modern sites, for assistance or information
- 3 modern loops offer a wide range of sites and scenery to choose from; to get away from it all, check out the 3 walk-in tenting sites at the beach
- see pages 28-29 for more information on camping

Picnic Shelter

- centrally located on the north side of the park within walking distance of the swimming beach and campgrounds
- large shelter with numerous tables, electric outlets and grills, available for reservations by calling the park; rental fee is a per-day charge (subject to change), plus an entrance fee for any vehicles
- surrounded by bur oak forest with open spaces for a wide range of activities
- playground, horseshoe pits and fishing dock

Picnic shelter

Amphitheater

Amphitheater

- located in south loop of modern campground
- site for most weekend evening interpretive programs
- available for presentations, church services and other programs; call park for availability and reservations
- built by Youth Conservation Corps in the 1970s

Fishing Dock

- located on northeast side of Lake Renwick, a short walk from the picnic shelter
- prepare for a steep hike down to dock, which has a high guard rail
- donated by Pembina County and Area Sportsmen's Club

ACTIVITIES

HIKING/BIKING TRAILS

As a child living along the Tongue River, G.B. Gunlogson loved to explore this riparian (floodplain) ecosystem consisting of wetlands, forests and oxbows. In order to move through this "jungle land," he followed a motley network of wildlife trails. Beginning in the summer of 1969 more extensive trails were developed on the south side of the newly established Gunlogson Nature Preserve. Today four individual trails crisscross the preserved area, taking visitors through a variety of landscapes.

Wildwood Trail (¾ mile)
- national recreation trail dedicated on August 25, 1978
- trail head located at the Gunlogson Barn
- interpretive trail with 25 sites describing aspects of this unique natural environment
- trail guide available that corresponds with numbered posts
- takes 45 minutes or more to hike and explore

Shady Springs Trail (1/2 mile)
- connects with Wildwood Trail at site 25
- trail moves along Tongue River through a wetland and back into upper prairie sections
- check out observation platform for beaver activity

Basswood Trail (1 1/2 miles)
- starts at metal bridge crossing Tongue River
- follow trail as it twists and turns near the river and among many large American basswoods
- terrain mostly level with a few slight depressions; watch for water on sections near wetlands

Trail head sign

Old Settlers Trail (3 miles)

- created in 1992; access via Basswood Trail or parking lot at the Renwick Dam
- follows a section of old oxcart trails through aspen woodlands and native prairie
- one steep hillside to tackle

Cav-landic Bike Trail

This non-motorized trail is a safe way for bikers, walkers, joggers and in-line skaters of all ages and abilities to travel back and forth between the park and Cavalier.

Features 6-mile paved trail that is 8.5 feet wide and located along the Department of Transportation right-of-way. It runs from the west edge of Cavalier to the Cavalier Golf Course.

Built with donations and through a Department of Transportation and a Symms Grant sponsored by the North Dakota Parks and Recreation Department.

Bike Trails

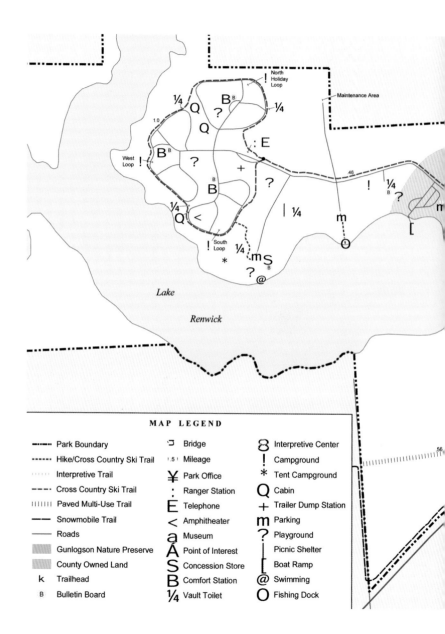

North
Holiday
Loop

Maintenance Area

¼ Q ? B ᴮ ¼

1.0 Q

B ᴮ E
West
Loop ? +
B ? 46 ! ¼
ᴮ ?
B ?

¼ ¼ m
Q < [
South
Loop ! ¼ O
* m S
? ᴮ
@

Lake

Renwick

MAP LEGEND

--⋅⋅⋅--	Park Boundary	⊃	Bridge	꒺	Interpretive Center
⋅⋅⋅⋅⋅⋅	Hike/Cross Country Ski Trail	.5	Mileage	!	Campground
⋅⋅⋅⋅⋅⋅	Interpretive Trail	¥	Park Office	*	Tent Campground
-----	Cross Country Ski Trail	⋮	Ranger Station	Q	Cabin
ⅠⅠⅠⅠⅠⅠ	Paved Multi-Use Trail	E	Telephone	+	Trailer Dump Station
──	Snowmobile Trail	<	Amphitheater	m	Parking
──	Roads	a	Museum	?	Playground
▨	Gunlogson Nature Preserve	Å	Point of Interest	Ⓛ	Picnic Shelter
▨	County Owned Land	S	Concession Store	[	Boat Ramp
k	Trailhead	B	Comfort Station	@	Swimming
B	Bulletin Board	¼	Vault Toilet	O	Fishing Dock

56

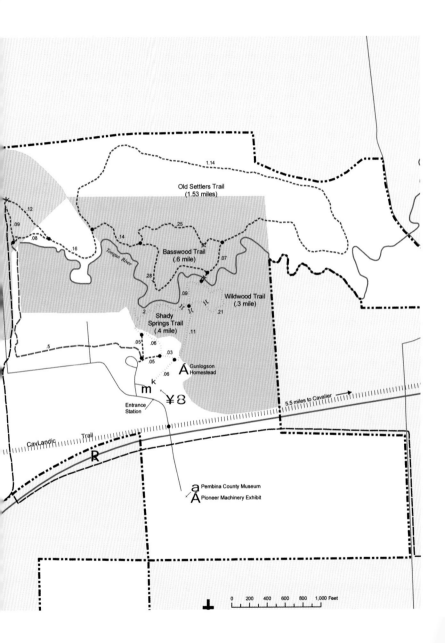

SWIMMING
Beach and Concessions at Lake Renwick

A gently-sloping, sandy swimming beach is one of the park's most popular spots. Expect a full parking lot on most warm weekends.

- designated swimming beach marked with buoys and rope; please respect all rules and regulations

- no lifeguard on duty; rescue equipment available at beach

Swimming Beach

- full-service concession available from mid-May through Labor Day
- available for sale: ice cream, pizza, candy, pop and sandwiches
- canoes and paddleboats for rent
- concession building includes bathrooms, changing rooms and showers
- volleyball court, playground equipment, picnic tables and grills

FISHING

Lake Renwick provides fishing opportunities both from shore and on the water. Check out the fishing dock located on the northeast corner of the lake or try your luck in the backwaters. Fish species include northern pike, yellow perch, crappies and walleyes.

Boat Ramp
- located on the northeast corner of lake near Renwick Dam
- wide concrete ramp with slight slope
- courtesy dock available for loading and unloading boats
- large parking lot
- lake and ramp closed to all boats at dusk

CAMPING
Sleeping Cabins
- 3 semi-modern cabins to rent mid-May to end of September

- one located in each of the 3 modern campground loops
- each sleeps 4–5 people, has lights, heat, fan and electricity
- outside fire ring and picnic table for cooking
- cost is a per-night (fee subject to change), plus entrance fee for vehicles

Modern Campground
- west, south and north loops
- 132 modern single-unit sites
- 8 modern group sites
- one comfort station in each loop with hot showers and flush toilets
- 50-amp service available
- sewer dump station
- telephone at ranger station
- playgrounds near all three loops
- amphitheater in south loop

Primitive Loop
- consists of 10 single primitive sites, 4 can be reserved in summer
- vault toilet and water hydrant
- overlooks Lake Renwick, short walk from Gunlogson Nature Preserve

Beach Loop Tent Area
- 3 single walk-in primitive sites west of concession area
- vault toilet and water hydrant

Information
- full service from mid-May through end of September
- south modern loop sites can be reserved all summer
- north modern loop sites can be reserved during major holidays

North campground

- call 1-800-807-4723; reservation line typically opens on first Tuesday of April; reservations can now be made online at www.parkrec.nd.gov
- please do not camp on sites marked "Reserved" unless you have a reservation or have consulted a park ranger
- 30-and 50-amp electrical hookups
- firewood available from campground host or a park employee

WINTER ACTIVITIES

Icelandic State Park takes on a whole new flavor during the winter. After the snow begins to fall, visitors have the opportunity to strap on a pair of cross-country skis to try out the well-protected and groomed trails in the Gunlogson Nature Preserve. Once the ice thickens, Lake Renwick becomes a small village of fish houses. Other activities include sledding at the primitive campground, enjoying the annual Christmas Event at the Pioneer Heritage Center, or doing a little bird watching. Outside the park there is downhill skiing at Frost Fire Mountain and snowmobiling along the Rendezvous Region trail system.

Cross-Country Skiing

Over 3 miles of trails are groomed regularly in the Gunlogson Nature Preserve. Most of it is nestled in the Tongue River Valley and protected from cold winter winds.

The majority of the terrain is fairly level with some slight depressions. At each end of the trail there is a challenging hill, along with one on the Old Settlers Trail.

You can start at the parking lots of either the Pioneer Heritage Center or Renwick Dam.

Cross-country skiing in the Gunlogson Nature Preserve

Maps are available for this trail system. Park staff may also groom a trail through the campground. Check with the park staff for trail conditions or view them at www.ndparks.com.

Ice Fishing On Lake Renwick

A popular sport for all ages. Whether you enjoy sitting out in the fresh air or hunkering inside a fish house, there is plenty of room for ice fishing on Lake Renwick. Park staff plow a road on the lake from the boat ramp to a turn-around area near the swimming beach.

Ice fishing is for all ages

In February an ice-fishing derby is held for both kids and adults. Sponsored by the Pembina County and Area Sportsmen's Club. Derby begins at 8 am and ends at 3 pm.

Please have all fish houses off the ice by March 1.

Other Winter Activities

In addition to the activities listed below, see page 35 for information about the Christmas Bird Count, Snowmobile Radar Run and Ice Fishing Derby.

- warming house located at primitive campground overlooking boat ramp and sledding hill—a popular spot on weekends and during the Christmas holiday
- opportunities for winter camping, snowshoeing and wildlife watching
- Pioneer Heritage Center is open year-round and hosts a Christmas event and Visitor Appreciation Day on the Sunday before Thanksgiving

Winter camping is fun, as long as you come prepared

EVENTS/PROGRAMS

Special events (both large and small) are an important part of Icelandic State Park and take place throughout the year. One of the most popular is the Kids Weekend in August, which celebrates a unique aspect of the park. Many other events are held annually—such as National Trails Day, Pioneer Machinery Day and Christmas in July. Winter is also a busy time at the park, with a number of smaller events like the Christmas Open House, Lake Renwick Fishing Derby, Snowmobile Radar Run and Christmas Bird Count.

Iron Kid Contest

SPECIAL EVENTS

Kids Weekend

If you are under the age of 15, or the parent of someone who is, this is your weekend. For one weekend each summer, Icelandic State Park is completely devoted to the whims and delights of children. Be prepared for a wide selection of activities and games, and reserve a campsite early.

Fun at Kids Weekend

Date second weekend of August
Hours Friday evening–Sunday afternoon
Friday Activities scavenger hunt, ice cream social and movie
Saturday Activities iron kid contest, arts and crafts fair and amphitheater program featuring a wide range of performers
Sunday Activities fishing derby, bike parade, and sand castle contest

National Trails Day

From the very beginning of this national event in 1993, Icelandic State Park has hosted a variety of hikes and programs. Visitors can enjoy one of the hikes guided by park staff or walk the trails on their own.

Date first Saturday in June which is also Visitor Appreciation Day, (entrance fee is waived)

Activities A hike on the Bluebird Trail is held to give visitors a chance to see newly hatched chicks. In the afternoon, take a stroll with a park naturalist on the Wildwood Trail. And at the end of your day, consider taking part in a night hike, focusing on all five senses.

Pioneer Machinery Show

Celebrate how farming was once done at a historical site filled with turn-of-the century buildings, exhibits and machinery displays. Volunteers will make you feel at home and gladly accept your offer to help (literally) as they demonstrate grain threshing, wheat grinding, shingle making, flail threshing and more.

Date Sunday after Labor Day Weekend

Hours 7–5

Activities Start with a pancake, sausage and French toast breakfast, served until 1 pm. The machinery parade begins at 1:15 pm, featuring antique tractors, trucks, cars and assorted farm implements. There is also an antique tractor pull, toy machinery show, crafts, flea market and food concessions.

Machinery parade

Christmas In July

Bring a little holiday cheer to the middle of summer by decorating your camper and campsite. Prizes will be awarded for "Best Lights," "Best Decked Site" and "People's Choice."

Date last full weekend of July

Activities In addition to the decorating contest, there is also ornament making, a coloring contest, guessing contests and holiday movies. On Saturday evening there is a bike parade led by Santa Claus.

Christmas in July celebration

Christmas Open House

Enjoy the Pioneer Heritage Center filled with Christmas trees, lights and holiday items. During the afternoon, listen to a variety of entertainers perform numerous Christmas songs.

Date Sunday before Thanksgiving

Hours noon–5

Activities horse-drawn rides available during the afternoon; cake and cider served throughout the event

WINTER SPECIAL EVENTS

Visitation is fairly low at Icelandic State Park during the winter, but it is still a great chance to participate in a number of special events.

Christmas Bird Count

Held one weekday during the holiday break. Park staff and volunteers travel a circle 15 miles in diameter counting all birds they see. The day begins at sunrise and ends at sunset. It is part of a national bird count.

Snowmobile Radar Run

A racing strip is cleaned off of Lake Renwick and hundreds of snowmobiles battle each other for top speed. Typically held in January or February.

Snowmobile Radar Run

Ice Fishing Derby

Join kids and adults from 8 am to 3 pm as they try their luck catching a northern or perch. This event is generally held at the beginning of February and is open to all.

INTERPRETIVE PROGRAMS

- held during summer from mid-May through Labor Day weekend

- on major holiday weekends, including July 4th, evening programs are also offered Sunday nights

- check for types of programs, times and other important

American Indian program at amphitheater

information in the weekend flyer, which is available at the entrance station or Pioneer Heritage Center

Evening Programs

- generally held on Friday and Saturday evenings at the amphitheater located in south campground between sites 82 and 83

- programs usually start at dusk, depending on whether a video is being shown

- look for special guest speakers at evening programs

- park amphitheater is surrounded by a thick planting of conifers and deciduous trees

Nature Hikes

Nature hike

- typically held on Sunday mornings starting at 10

- hikes usually held on a nature trail in the Gunlogson Nature Preserve

- be prepared for mosquitoes, uneven terrain and variety of weather

- hikes usually last 45 minutes to an hour

Dakota Adventure

- offered for children ages 7–12 to explore the natural environment through a wide range of hands-on activities

- programs have ranged from wilderness survival to beaver ecology

- usually held Saturday mornings from 10–noon

- meet interpreters at picnic shelter unless otherwise noted

Bald eagle demonstration

EVENTS/PROGRAMS

NATURE

At one time Icelandic State Park was covered by glacial Lake Agassiz, which is still evident by the sand and gravel deposits of its former beach. In presettlement days this area was on the western edge of the tallgrass prairie. Today remnants of native grasses, forbs and flowers are still found scattered in the park. Natural woodlands survive along the Tongue River riparian (floodplain) corridor and Lake Renwick. This natural area is home to an interesting selection of birds, animals and plants.

GEOLOGY

Flowing out of the north, a series of glaciers shaped the landscape of Icelandic State Park. It began a million years ago when the climate grew colder and snow piled up and slowly compacted into ice. This massive sheet of ice moved south, retreated with warmer temperatures and then began to move outward once again. North Dakota had at least two glaciers slide through this part of the state and possibly four of them.

As the last glacier began to melt, the water had no place to go and began to form Lake Agassiz, a massive inland sea. Finally an outlet was created northeast of the park, pushing the melting ice toward Hudson Bay. Present-day rivers like the Tongue and Pembina started to carve their way eastward to the Red River. These relatively young rivers haven't had time to establish deep channels and are susceptible to flooding.

Beach ridge of former Lake Agassiz under the cover of snow and below the Gunlogson Barn.

ECOSYSTEM
Tallgrass Prairie

Unique to North America, this ecosystem spread over a million acres from the Gulf of Mexico into the northern reaches of Canada. It extended east from the state of Indiana to the foothills of the Rocky Mountains. It flourished just 170 years ago, until a wave of settlers transformed the prairie into a productive agricultural landscape.

The history of the tallgrass prairie can be traced back to around 8,000 years ago as the last glacier receded. Warmer temperatures and drier conditions favored this grassland ecosystem over the retreating woodlands. A variety of factors ranging from soils, moisture capacity, rainfall, evaporation rate and summer drought played a role in the development of the tallgrass prairie.

Throughout Icelandic State Park, visitors can find scattered remnants of tallgrass and sand prairies. On the well-drained soils you can still discover native grasses like big bluestem and Indian grass or the forbs of milkweed or leadplant, along with wildflowers like coneflowers and wild prairie rose.

Yellow coneflower

GUNLOGSON NATURE PRESERVE

The Gunlogson Nature Preserve is a great, secluded spot to visit and explore, and a wonderful place to escape from everyday life . On a hot and windy day this is the perfect location to find a cool and moist climate. You will have a choice of hiking one or all of the four trails, moving among towering basswoods, along a meandering Tongue River and through open areas filled with native grasses and wildflowers.

G.B. Gunlogson in Gunlogson Nature Preserve

Five different natural communities are found in the Gunlogson Nature Preserve, including two forested areas, the river, wetlands and a mixed-grass prairie. Each plays a role in the type of plants that grow there and the wildlife attracted to this particular landscape. The forest and wetland habitats are significant biological features that represent a link to an earlier time and climate conditions not seen here today.

Lowland Woodland

As the prevailing community type, it occupies all but the wettest areas in the Tongue River floodplain. Look for a dominance of eastern deciduous forest species, including basswood, ironwood, green ash and boxelder.

Trail through wetland via plank bridge

A shrub layer dominated by beaked hazel is found under the forest canopy on well-drained soils and in openings among mature trees. Other shrubs include the speckled alder, Juneberry, red osier dogwood and chokecherry. There is also a variety of plants found here like moonseed, woodbine, woodland rose, wild grape and, of course, poison ivy.

"Enter this wild wood and view the haunts of nature. This Arboretum tells a living story about how the land was formed by glaciers, water, wind, plant growth and time. These forces leveled the upland, carved out the river bottom, sorted out soil types and created a wide variety of ecological situations that harbor different kinds of trees, shrubs, grasses, wildflowers and pond life in their special haunts or adaptations for life," wrote G.B. Gunlogson.

Trails moves off upper prairie plateau into a floodplain zone

Oak Woodland

Found on the upper margins of the Tongue River Valley, bur oak dominates this community type. On the steep north-facing valley slopes there is a mixture of aspen, paper birch and green ash, along with a selection of northern shrubs and herbs.

Across the river, bur oaks are more widely spaced out in a savanna-type atmosphere, intermixed with native grasses and wildflowers. This area had been grazed for many years, is drier and the trees are younger.

River And Creeks

The Tongue River is one of several small streams flowing eastward from the higher elevation of the Pembina Hills into the Red River. Due to its recent geologic origin, this stream's drainage pattern is relatively new and indefinite. As glacial Lake Agassiz dried up, the Red River became the main outlet for the Tongue.

After construction of the Renwick Dam, this segment of the river has changed a good deal due to the sediment load being dumped upstream in the reservoir. Today the plants in the riparian (shoreside) area don't benefit from annual flooding and the spreading of new soil layer.

This section of the river is spring-fed and reaches a low flow by the end of summer, but won't run dry. Due to the river flowing year-round it maintains a stable aquatic community. The

Tongue River during spring flooding

Tongue River is a vital component to the Gunlogson Nature Preserve and has been identified as a system of biological significance at the state, regional and local levels.

"The changes in the seasons were inspirational experiences. The grandest and most exciting of all was the coming of spring, which would fill our senses with a symphony of sounds and colors and a feeling of aliveness. Then slowly the soft songs of summer and the drone of bumble bees would take over to soothe our senses, and provide a delightful interlude before the coming of autumn and the more dramatic changes that followed," wrote G. B. Gunlogson.

Wetland Thicket

This is thought to represent a "relic community" dating back to a time when the area's climate was cooler and moister. It was a period when forest plants and animals moved into the area in the wake of the glaciers and the subsequent retreat of Lake Agassiz.

There are four major wetland thicket basins scattered in and around the Gunlogson Nature Preserve. Today they maintain the highest local concentrations of rare species, including water arum, lady's fern, bishop's cap, meadow horsetail and spinulose shield.

This community type has also been called a swamp, shrub carr, alder thicket and a marsh. It is spring-fed, remains saturated year-round, and depends on stable groundwater flow to the surface. Dense shrubs of alder, with both eastern deciduous and boreal aquatic species present,

Marsh marigold blooming in a wetland

dominate these wetland thickets, although many of these plants are found at the outer limits of their range.

Native grasses

Mixed-Grass Prairie

The final community type found in the Gunlogson Nature Preserve, it is a small remnant of what was once the most extensive plant community in North Dakota. It is commonly referred to as a savanna ecosystem.

Although it has been disturbed because of grazing, you can still find big bluestem, little bluestem, dropseed, needle-and-thread grass and Junegrass. There is also an abundance of herbaceous flowering plants, with very few trees and shrubs.

Lake Renwick

LAKE RENWICK

Formed in the early 1960s with the construction of the Renwick Dam on the Tongue River, the lake provides flood control and recreational activities to the local residents and visitors. It was the last in a series of seven dams built in the region by the federal government's Small Watershed Program after a number of devastating floods in the late 1940s and early '50s. In 1959 the Pembina County Water Management Board purchased 500 acres to construct the dam. Lake Renwick became one of the largest dams in the county, retaining 1,160 acre feet or 35 million gallons of water. Lake Renwick is a popular spot for speedboats, water-skiers, swimmers and anglers. See page 28 for more details.

Information

Size 220-acre manmade reservoir, approximately 1.25 miles long and 1/4 mile wide, with 5 miles of shoreline and 989 feet above sea level

Built 1959–1962

Paddling on Lake Renwick

Facilities boat ramp, courtesy dock, fishing dock not accessible for those with physical challenges, swimming area, concession, changing rooms and bathrooms

Fish walleyes, crappies, perch and northern pike

The Tongue River Pilot Project became one of the first watershed projects in the nation. When this project was completed 11 years later, a series of dams provided efficient water control.

NATURE

NATURE CHECKLISTS

The Gunlogson Nature Preserve is the ideal location for bird watching and finding a broad selection of trees and flowers. A number of less-traveled spots are located along the western edge of Lake Renwick; also check out the conifer forest established by the park staff. Head over to the Pembina Gorge and Jay V. Wessels Wildlife Management Area for additional wildlife watching.

Birds

Dominated by heavily forested sections, the Gunlogson Nature Preserve is perfect for bird watching and provides additional habitats ranging from wetlands to open meadows. You will be able to find a number of rare and endangered species, including the pileated woodpecker.

Bald eagle

Here are a few of the many birds you can find at Icelandic State Park. See how many you can find!

☐ American woodcock
☐ Canada goose
☐ common loon
☐ common yellowthroat
☐ Cooper's hawk
☐ mountain bluebird
☐ eastern bluebird
☐ northern waterthrush
☐ osprey

☐ ovenbird
☐ pileated woodpecker
☐ purple finch
☐ red-breasted nuthatch
☐ red-winged blackbird
☐ ruby-throated hummingbird
☐ scarlet tanager
☐ western grebe
☐ yellow-rumped warbler

NATURE

Mammals/Reptiles

There are plenty of opportunities for spotting a variety of animals, especially in the off-season when the park is fairly quiet. Walking the various nature trails at dusk or dawn will give you the greatest opportunity for observing wildlife up close.

White-tailed deer

There are a number of animals at Icelandic. Try your luck at spotting them!

☐ beaver
☐ coyote
☐ gray squirrel
☐ leopard frog
☐ long-tailed weasel
☐ moose
☐ painted turtle
☐ raccoon

☐ red squirrel
☐ smooth green snake
☐ snapping turtle
☐ snowshoe hare
☐ striped skunk
☐ tiger salamander
☐ white-tailed deer
☐ woodchuck

Big bluestem

Plants

Icelandic's wide variety of prairie, forest and wetland ecosystems offer the chance to identify a mixture of flowers, forbs, grasses, shrubs and trees. Check off each plant as you find it!

For more information:
Flora of the Great Plains by members of the Great Plains Flora Assoc.
Wildflowers of North Dakota by Paul Kannowski

- ☐ Allegheny monkey-flower
- ☐ basswood
- ☐ beaked hazel
- ☐ big bluestem
- ☐ black-eyed Susan
- ☐ blazing star
- ☐ bur oak
- ☐ crested fern
- ☐ chokecherry
- ☐ duckweed
- ☐ enchanter's nightshade
- ☐ false Solomon's seal
- ☐ fringed loosestrife
- ☐ gray goldenrod
- ☐ green ash
- ☐ hawthorn
- ☐ horsetail
- ☐ Indian grass
- ☐ ironwood
- ☐ Joe-pye weed
- ☐ Juneberry
- ☐ Kentucky bluegrass
- ☐ lady's fern

- ☐ long-leaved stitchwort
- ☐ marsh marigold
- ☐ meadow horsetail
- ☐ needle-and-thread
- ☐ northern bedstraw
- ☐ ostrich fern
- ☐ pasque flower
- ☐ paper birch
- ☐ red osier dogwood
- ☐ Russian thistle
- ☐ small bellwort
- ☐ southern watermeal
- ☐ stiff sunflower
- ☐ touch-me-not
- ☐ two-seeded sedge
- ☐ Virginia creeper
- ☐ wild grape
- ☐ wild mint
- ☐ wild prairie rose
- ☐ wild raspberry
- ☐ wolfberry
- ☐ yarrow

HISTORY

Two distinctive forces established Icelandic State Park in the early 1960s. It started with the construction of Renwick Dam to control flooding along the Tongue River. A 220-acre lake and the surrounding land were first developed as a recreational area by Pembina County's Water Management Board. In 1964 the park was created from the donation of the Gunlogson homestead and the recreational area. Since then the park has seen immense increase in development and visitation. In 1989, the Pioneer Heritage Center was built and today there are a number of restored historical buildings.

THE BEGINNING

In 1964, G.B. Gunlogson and his sister Loa donated their parents' homestead and 200 acres to the state of North Dakota, helping to create Icelandic State Park.

"Offers to buy this land have come to me from time to time. But, to me there are certain intangible values, such as echo of the whippoorwill which no buyer could be expected to pay for and which he might not even appreciate. So I had decided long ago that it should never be sold. Instead, it has been my intention to turn this land over to such purposes as might be of the greatest value to the community and the state," wrote Gunlogson.

On August 2, 1964, thousands of people faced a platform along the shores of Lake Renwick to hear the state formally dedicate Icelandic State Park. "Icelandic" came about because a few key people in Pembina County wanted to give proper recognition to immigrants from this western European country. During the first 10 years, progress on the park was slow or nonexistent. Most of this had to do with a lack of funds and little effort on part of the North Dakota Park Service. Until 1975, when the department hired the park's first superintendent, it was managed as a seasonal operation.

Even though there wasn't much support from Bismarck, Icelandic saw a number of important projects completed during the first decade. National Guard units helped provide a few basic visitor facilities, including road development, improvement of a boat ramp and the construction of picnic areas. In the late 1960s the park hosted two important Pembina County celebrations; more than 4,000 people attended the county's centennial event.

Progress continued to move forward in 1970 with the construction of the first modern campground. It included a full-service comfort station and 50 sites with electric and water hookups. As the park's popularity and visitation continued to

G.B. Gunlogson at dedication of Gunlogson National Recreation Trail

grow, a second modern campground was added in 1980. Other facilities built during this time featured an amphitheater, shop/office building, ranger station and a park manager's residence.

Other key developments at Icelandic State Park were being completed on the Gunlogson land. Along the Tongue River, trails were carved and improved throughout the 1970s. One of them, Wildwood Trail, received a National Recreation designation in 1978. This self-guided trail gave visitors the opportunity to learn about the area's history, plants, geology and wildlife. In 1983 the 200-acre donation was honored as the first nature preserve in North Dakota. It is home to a number of rare plant and animal species, including the southern watermeal and pileated woodpecker. Today four trails provide a place for people to hike, observe wildlife and ski.

1980S AND NORTHEASTERN NORTH DAKOTA HERITAGE ASSOCIATION

Icelandic State Park's progress began to take huge leaps in the '80s when local residents took a more active role in its development. After a fleeting attempt to establish a citizens' group, the Northeastern North Dakota

Heritage Association was formed in 1986. The goal of this group was to build a heritage center to interpret the pioneer homestead era of 1870 to 1920. With an outpouring of dedication, hard work and donations, the group accomplished many of its goals and dreams.

Heritage association meeting

On July 4, 1989, the Northeastern North Dakota Heritage Association saw its first dream come true when the Pioneer Heritage Center opened its doors to the public. This interpretive center tells the story about the life and achievements of the first settlers, their ethnic and cultural diversity, the difficulty in settling the land, the climactic hazards they faced, the significance of religion and education, their perseverance and self-sufficiency, and their remarkable progress. The Heritage Association continues to move forward with their goal of telling the "North Dakota Story" through restoration of historic buildings, the creation of exhibits and hosting special events.

The Cranley School became the first historic building moved onto the site; it was restored and dedicated in 1992. This one-room building represents the 100-plus country schools that once served the children of Pembina County. Next came the Akra Hall, built for community events by a local chapter of the Modern Woodmen of America. By 1995 the Hallson Church had been moved into the park. This Icelandic Lutheran Church was one of the last buildings left standing in Hallson. The last component, a log cabin, was constructed by volunteers.

Cranley School being restored

Across from the Pioneer Heritage Complex is another important historical interpretive site. The Pioneer Machinery Site has been developed to display the agricultural equipment of the past and tell the story of the people who used it. Over the last 10 years progress has been made with the restoration of the Bathgate Depot, two large display buildings were built, and four more historic buildings—McKechnie Granary, Stegman Barn and Blacksmith Shop, Patton House and a blacksmith building—have been added. After the new Pembina County Museum was constructed, the St. Anthony Catholic Church was moved here as well.

G.B. GUNLOGSON

This son of Icelandic immigrants grew up on his parents' homestead at the turn of the century, along with two brothers, Carl and John, and two sisters, Thorstina and Loa. "All of us deeply loved this home. We were also blessed by living in a delightful community, a sublime example of what the early settlers had achieved, notwithstanding poverty and great physical hardships," wrote G.B. Gunlogson later in his life.

G.B. Gunlogson

Family Homestead

When G.B. was born in 1887 the family still lived in the log cabin his father had built seven years earlier. It was a hard existence for the family, with everyone helping out as they struggled to make a living. Despite the hardship of living on the frontier, Eggert built one of the first two-story frame houses in the area. Their farm became a stopping place for people traveling through to stake their own claim, to purchase supplies or for those looking for a place to stay. For G.B. these visitors opened a whole new world, one that was just beyond the horizon.

As a small boy, G.B. showed early signs of mechanical aptitude, as well as a fondness for nature. The young lad was never happier than when he was either working on machinery or roaming the woods along the Tongue River. Oaks, elms, basswood, shrubbery and a multitude of colorful flowers were growing there and it felt like an oasis compared to the adjoining flat, treeless plains. The natural world provided a wonderful contrast, with the cool shade and dappled woodland along the river, surrounded by the hot, windy plains.

G.B.'s Education

His formal education began in Akra's one-room schoolhouse, just a mile from the farm. But this wasn't enough for G.B., who read as many books as he could get. After graduating from the eighth grade, G.B. left home to continue his education. "Laugi" had just been confirmed at the Vildrain Lutheran Church, and it was the pastor who suggested a boy possessing such a keen mind should go on to an institution of higher learning, where his unusual talents might be developed. In the fall, he started out for Luther College in Decorah, Iowa.

As a youth, plowing behind a team of oxen for 10 hours a day with nothing to do but think and dream, it was only natural for G.B. to think about ways to reduce the drudgery and increase production.

"My interest in inventions and new developments began early. When I learned to plow with oxen, I began to dream about replacing work animals with mechanical power."

G.B. worked at a succession of jobs, including carpentry and clearing brush to put himself through engineering courses.

"I attended a country school and later taught a few terms in the country. My college career was somewhat sporadic because of lack of funds and part-time jobs to pay expenses. The college bookstore became a source of information. I began to acquire textbooks on science and technology in various fields and I have tried to keep up with the progress in science and engineering ever since."

The choice of engineering as a career was both inevitable and logical for G.B. Gunlogson. There were roads and bridges to build, lands to be drained and reclaimed. "Although as I have learned in later years, much of that work should have been left to the beavers. They have shown better sense of land use than some engineers."

Gunlogson Homestead

G.B.'s Professional Career

G.B.'s first "full-time" engineering job was as a surveyor when he and a friend opened a partnership in Fargo. After a number of months saw few jobs, they decided that one of the partners should get a temporary job.

"So I got a job with the J.I. Case Threshing Machine Co.," G.B. recalled, "but only for the summer. Yet month by month I found the work more and more interesting and the Case organization more congenial. Promotions began to come along and it became increasingly difficult to leave the interesting work I found with Case."

At age 22, G.B. went off to Racine, Wisconsin, to take a position in product development. Throughout his life he was never pinned down to a desk job working on someone else's ideas. He was the developer—an idea man. During his varied career with Case, G.B. worked as a research engineer, as advertising and sales promotion manager and as the first head of the J.I. Case Motor Car Division.

In 1925, after a 16-year career with Case, Gunlogson joined the advertising department of the Western Printing Company in Racine. His interest in advertising grew from the knowledge that most farmers were unaware of the great labor-saving

G.B Gunlogson at his desk

advances in farm technology. Later he formed his own company, the Western Advertising Agency and carved out a notable career for himself. After 35 years in the advertising business, G.B. retired upon the sale of his company.

Gunlogson Nature Preserve

In the late '40s and '50s, G.B. began to work on establishing a nature sanctuary on his family's homestead for education and research. He laid out carefully prepared plans for all those interested in the nature project and hoped this tract of land would be used as "an experiment in education."

"What we are contemplating here," G.B. said, "is perhaps, less a research than it is an educational project. To make their life on earth more worthwhile, the individual needs to be on good terms not only with their human neighbors, their automobile, radio and good books, but also with the natural environment about them, the earth which nurtures them and the plants and animals which share it with them. If education is to contribute to their better life, it must come as well from a deeper understanding and appreciation of the beauties and processing in living nature as from study of the humanities and arts.

"The 200 acres consist of a varied terrain of woods, old fields, grass-lands, river and wilderness remnants. It harbors nearly every species of wildlife native to North Dakota. Permitting the land to revert to its original, undisturbed natural status, ecologists say will serve science in many ways.

"School children and other youth groups will find there an excellent opportunity to study and become acquainted with most of the plants, birds and wildlife to be found in the state. Many societies, with an interest in natural science, as well as conservationists will have in this sanctuary an opportunity to study these birds, plants, insects, flowers in their natural habitat and in time the area should provide a living record of North Dakota as it was in the beginning."

This generous act of G.B. was not a result of some sudden impulse; it was an act of conservation. G.B. continued to support the preservation of his family's homestead for future generations and the establishment of Icelandic State Park. After his death in 1983 at the age of 96,

G.B. Gunlogson and Governor Art Link at the dedication of Gunlogson Nature Preserve and ISP

his widow, Esther, continued this dedication for the development of both the homestead and park. Until her death in 1994, Esther Gunlogson was a major supporter of the Northeastern North Dakota Heritage Association, donating funds for the Pioneer Heritage Center Complex.

PEMBINA GORGE

A beautiful, undeveloped river valley extending from Manitoba northwest of Icelandic State Park is home to the Pembina River. One of North Dakota's deepest and steepest river valleys, the Pembina Gorge is open for visitors to explore and view a variety of wildlife and plants. Today it encompasses the largest uninterrupted block of woodlands in the state, about 12,500 acres, along with scattered grasslands. Visitors enjoy downhill skiing, golfing, fossil hunting, snowmobiling, canoeing, community plays, bird watching and much more. The Pembina Gorge is called the "Valley of the Gods."

Pembina River

Location/Directions Northwest of Walhalla the land is owned by private individuals along with the state Game and Fish and Parks and Recreation departments. From Walhalla, go 5 miles west on Co. 55. Turn north and go for 1 mile; turn west, then follow the winding road to wildlife management areas on the Pembina and Little North Pembina rivers.

The Rendezvous Region Snowmobile Trail System will take you to the Pembina Gorge or into Minnesota. Today, the North Dakota Parks and Recreation Department is working to establish a year-round trail system in the Pembina Gorge.

Concerns beware of adverse gravel road conditions, especially when wet from rain or snow
Website http://tradecorridor.com/walhalla/attractions.htm

Nature

The heavily forested areas are intermixed with croplands, hayfields, marshes, bogs and small lakes. Trees include quaking aspen, bur oak, American elm, basswood and green ash. More than 480 species of plants have been identified, including 30 species rare to the state.

Moose are a common sight in the Pembina Gorge

Birds And Wildlife

Viewing opportunities in the Pembina Gorge include driving, hiking and canoeing. There is a 22-mile (round-trip) route for observing a variety of birds and wildlife. Birds include pileated woodpeckers, indigo buntings, American redstarts, orange-crowned warblers and wild turkeys.

The Pembina Gorge is known for its large number of moose and North Dakota's only naturally occurring elk population. Other animals you may see include beaver and white-tailed deer.

Gravel road running through the Pembina Gorge

Snowmobiling

Over 450 miles of trails make up the Pembina Gorge Trail System. The trails are groomed on a regular basis depending on snow conditions. Originally developed by the Northeast Snowmobile Club, the system has numerous warming houses on the trails. The club sponsors "The Snowfest," an annual ride held on Martin Luther King weekend.

Contact Pembina Hills Trail Riders Snowmobile Club of Walhalla, PO Box 825, Walhalla, ND 58282; PembinaHillsTrailriders@hotmail.com

FROST FIRE MOUNTAIN SKI RESORT AND SUMMER THEATER

Situated in the heart of the Pembina Gorge, this family-owned business is unique to North Dakota. Visitors can enjoy downhill skiing and snowboarding in winter, and in summer the hills are filled with the sights and sounds of Summer Stock Theater.

Ski Resort

Ten ski runs with several 2,000-foot stretches are serviced by two chair lifts and one tow rope. The longest run is 2,600', vertical drop 350', and elevation is 1,350. A large comfortable lodge hosts a ski

Frost Fire Mountain

rental shop, snack area and lounge, along with a cafeteria and dining room. Other features include a half pipe for snowboarders, terrain park, ski lessons and a volunteer ski patrol. The resort traditionally opens on Thanksgiving.

Location 7 miles west of Walhalla on Hwy. 55
Contact 701-549-3600; www.frostfireskiarea.com

Summer Theater

Running from the end of June to the beginning of August, this well-designed outdoor amphitheater features a popular selection of musicals and plays. A dinner buffet in the barn is served on Saturday and Sunday. There is also a Victorian house selling local arts and crafts. Classic plays have ranged from *Annie Get Your Gun* to *Fiddler on the Roof* to *Forever Plaid*.

Contact 701-549-3600; www.frostfiretheatre.com

TETRAULT WOODS STATE FOREST

On both sides of the Pembina River, visitors will find a trail system meandering through over 400 acres of state forest land. The Tetrault Woods is an ideal spot for hiking, wildlife viewing and enjoying a natural riparian (floodplain) forest highlighting a diversity of plant and animal life.

Located 1.5 miles south of Walhalla on Hwy. 32; can also be accessed a mile south of Co. 55

Activities hiking, birding, horseback riding, picnicking, cross-country skiing and snowmobiling

Size 432 acres

Established 1970

Management North Dakota Forest Service

Contact NDFS at 701-549-2441; Walhalla Area Chamber of Commerce at 701-549-3939; www.tradecorridor.com/walhalla

PEMBINA RIVER

Flowing out of Canada, two northern branches of the Pembina River join with the south branch west of Walhalla before meandering near the Canadian border all the way to the Red River at the city of Pembina. As North Dakota's

Paddling the Pembina River

only whitewater river, it has some challenging rapids west of Walhalla and mellower conditions as you float eastward. This secluded and tranquil area is also perfect for other activities such as wildlife watching, tubing, fishing and hunting.

Floating The Pembina River

- Pembina River meanders through thickly wooded slopes, broad uplands and onto the former bed of Lake Agassiz

- a rocky bed offers mild whitewater experiences; upstream of Walhalla there is a Class I rapids—this stretch recommended for intermediate paddlers

- best trip is along upper stretch of the Pembina River, from the Vang Bridge (Co. 55) in Cavalier County to Hwy. 32 Bridge near Walhalla or Riverside Park, both in Pembina County—trip takes approximately 2–4 hours and includes rapids and quick turns

- no specific canoe access points at the bridges, but access is good—beware of hazards including downed trees and snags

- flow information: check Neche gaging station (nd.water.usgs.gov)—recommended flow of at least 1000 cfs—or contact ND Forest Service (701-549-2441)

- timbered hills in river corridor provide a scenic background and unique flora and fauna

Pembina River rapids

Pembina River Sites

Old Numedahl Bridge This is the first put-in point for paddling the Pembina River as it flows into the United States from Canada. Unfortunately, due to minimally maintained roads, this can be a tough site to reach. From the east side of the Pembina River it means a 2-mile trip on a steep dirt road with large ruts and swampy sections. The site can be reached a little easier on the west side of the river by taking the first northern township road after the Vang Bridge.

Vang Bridge A perfect spot to put-in for a paddle on the Pembina; also a popular local landmark. The run from this bridge to Riverside Park is considered the most popular.

Tetrault Woods State Forest The Pembina River flows past this 432-acre tract with nature trails and opportunities for hiking, snowmobiling and cross-country skiing.

Riverside Park This city park provides a paddling access, modern and primitive camping, picnic area and comfort station. The Pembina River now begins to flatten out as it flows eastward toward the Red River. Paddlers should be prepared for downed trees blocking the river.

Pembina Park Here you will find a boat ramp, canoe access, primitive camping, picnic area, fire rings and comfort station. At the park check out the Pembina Historic Site, an early fur trading post.

JAY V. WESSELS WILDLIFE MANAGEMENT AREA

Yellow-headed blackbird

Rolling sandhills created from a delta of glacial Lake Agassiz are now covered by an oak and aspen forest, perfect for wildlife viewing and taking a break from reality. This wildlife area is managed by the North Dakota Game and Fish Department and a favorite project of the Pembina County and Area Sportsman's Club. A high water table and sandy soil provides a perfect location for wetland bogs.

Location/Directions West of Icelandic State Park among the Pembina Hills is a 3,300-acre mixture of forested and prairie sections set aside for wildlife conservation. This area starts on the south side of the gravel road and then borders both sides.

From Icelandic State Park head west on Hwy. 5 and turn north on Hwy. 32. Travel approximately 9 miles before turning east on gravel (97th Street NE) and travel 2.5 miles to the border of Jay V. Wessels.

Contact North Dakota Game and Fish at 701-328-6300

Wildlife

One of the best spots for finding moose in their favorite habitat, aspen-dominated forests, it is also ideal for viewing coyotes, wild turkeys, ruffed grouse and snowshoe hares.

Jay V. Wessels

Bird Watching

Look for orange-crowned, chestnut-sided and Nashville warblers, American redstarts, great crested flycatchers, American woodcock, ovenbirds, northern waterthrushes and mourning warblers.

Nature

Quaking aspen and bur oak dominate forested sections, along with a mixture of other deciduous trees and shrubs.

Activities

Include hiking, wildlife watching, cross-country skiing and horseback riding. Trails are undeveloped and not groomed.

HISTORIC SITES

Pembina State Museum

Located in the state's oldest permanent European settlement, visitors can explore exhibits on prehistoric cultures, the fur trade, Métis bison hunters, military forts, steamboats and a travel information center.

Location just off I-29 (exit 215) in the town of Pembina

Features a 7-story observation tower offering a panoramic view of the Red River Valley, in addition to permanent and temporary galleries, a meeting room, gift shop and interpretive programs

Contact 701-825-6840; www.nd.gov/hist

Pembina State Museum

Gingras State Historic Site

One of the most important historic sites in the Red River Valley. One of the most important historic sites in the Red River Valley, the site Includes trading post and 1840s home of Métis trader Antoine B. Gingras, located near the Canadian border.

Gingras building

From 1843 to 1873 this trading post served the Métis community in the northern Red River Valley. Listed on the National Register of Historic Places.

Location 1.5 miles NE of Walhalla on Hwy. 32
Hours Thurs–Mon 10–5; May 16–Sept 15
Contact State Historical Society; 701-549-2775; www.nd.gov/hist

Walhalla State Historic Site

This spots marks the birthplace of Walhalla, originally called St. Joseph. Today this site is also home to the Kittson Trading Post, built in 1851 on the edge of the Pembina Escarpment. The trading post is North Dakota's oldest building.

Walhalla State Historic Site

Location 3 blocks SW of Hwy. 32 and Co. 55 intersection in Walhalla
Hours open year-round
Facilities 2 log buildings, restrooms, picnic shelters, interpretive sign, hiking trails and parking lot

Oak Lawn Church State Historic Site

Site of a former log church, this structure was built in 1885 by a Presbyterian congregation. Over the years it was also used for Baptist and Methodist services. By 1910 services were no longer being held and in 1933 the State Historical Society of North Dakota took over management of the site. Unfortunately, a grass fire destroyed the church on November 6, 1954.

Location west of Icelandic State Park on Hwy. 5
Facilities fieldstone marker, cemetery and a tree grove
Contact 701-328-2666

Stone marker at Oak Lawn

RESOURCES

SUPPORT GROUPS

Pembina County Historical Society

A key support group for Icelandic State Park, this citizens' group was created in 1967 following Pembina County's centennial celebration. This group has been instrumental in collecting and interpreting the county's history and developing the Pioneer Machinery Site.

Accomplishments

1992 Bathgate Depot moved to site and restored

1994 first Pioneer Machinery Show is held

1997 22 acres of land purchased adjacent to park

1998 McKechnie Granary restored

1999 Stegman Barn moved to site and restored

2001 Pembina County Historical Museum is built

2004 St. Anthony Catholic Church is moved to site

Pembina Machinery Show

Goals

- receive, restore and collect equipment, tools, machinery and other artifacts, provide and develop displays for public view
- educate, by telling the story of artifacts and people who used them
- utilize skills with demonstrations and special exhibits
- preserve our history for future generations to see

Restoring of the McKechnie Granary

Northeastern North Dakota Heritage Association

Formed in the spring of 1986, this citizens' group works hand in hand with Icelandic State Park to preserve the heritage of the pioneer settlers of northeastern North Dakota. Originally, its goal was to raise money to build the Pioneer Heritage Center; since then it has grown to over 300 members throughout the United States. Today the Heritage Association continues to raise funds, develop exhibits, host special events, create landscape designs, greet visitors and conduct research.

Member Benefits

- $15.00 per person or an annual membership. Or you can choose the Life Membership plan; plan varies on the age and amount—please contact the park for a membership schedule

Dedication of the Pioneer Heritage Center

- free entrance to the Pioneer Heritage Complex and any special events sponsored by the NEND Heritage Association
- 2 issues of the Home Quarter newsletter, published in spring and fall
- board meetings once a month at 7 pm on third Thursday at Pioneer Heritage Center; a special guest speaker is a part of most meetings

Committees

- Exhibit and Research
- Special Events
- Publicity and Newsletter
- Landscaping
- School
- Church
- Gift Store

Contact Mike Olafson, P.O. Box 32, Edinburg, ND 58227; or the park

Project Milestones

1986 a group of people interested in preserving their heritage for future generations gathered at the Pembina County Courthouse, laying down the foundation for the NEND Heritage Association

1989 Pioneer Heritage Center is dedicated in July as part of the ND Centennial

1990 Cranley School becomes the first building placed on the Heritage Center grounds

1993 on September 15th the Akra Hall is moved to the park and restored; NEND Heritage Association passes the $600,000 level in fund raising

1994 a third building, Hallson Church, finds a new home at complex

Dedication of the Pioneer Log Cabin

1995 NEND Heritage Association is debt free after receiving $346,800 from the Gunlogson Living Trust

2000 construction of the Pioneer Log Cabin completed and dedicated

Special Events

- Christmas Open House
- Rendezvous Festival
- Pioneer Machinery Show
- Artists Festival
- many temporary exhibits and open houses

Music in the Akra Hall

Pembina County & Area Sportsman's Wildlife Club

This grassroots group of all volunteers strives in a variety of ways to improve wildlife habitat and numbers. Members have worked hard to protect everything from waterfowl to elk and set aside conservation areas. Projects have included assisting in the development of J.V. Wessels Wildlife Management Area, releasing ring-necked pheasants and building nesting sites for Canada geese.

Activities

- hosts an annual wildlife banquet in fall for fund raising
- maintains a shooting range along Highway 5 west of Icelandic State Park
- holds monthly meetings and annual Fishing Derby in February on Lake Renwick

Contact

Park Manager at Icelandic State Park, 13571 Hwy 5, Cavalier, ND 58220; 701-265-4561; isp@nd.gov

North Dakota Parks & Recreation Department

This mostly rural state is blessed with a system of 17 state parks and recreation areas, each offering something unique and special. Visitors will find amazing scenery, varied outdoor recreational amenities, important wildlife habitat, protection of cultural and natural resources, and tranquility that helps balance the stress of everyday life.

Contact

Headquarters
1600 Century Avenue
Bismarck, ND 58503
701-328-5357; parkrec@nd.gov
www.ndparks.com

Fishing Derby

INDEX

NOTES

NOTES

NOTES

NOTES

NOTES